BATTLEFIELDS
IN BRITAIN

BATTLEFIELDS IN BRITAIN

BY C. V. WEDGWOOD

UNIFORM
PRESS

Uniform Press Ltd
66 Charlotte Street
London
W1T 4QE

First published in 1944
Published by Uniform Press Ltd 2015

ISBN 978-1910065-19-8

Cover designed by Felicity Price-Smith
Insides designed by Tora Kelly
Printed in India by Imprint Digital.

CONTENTS

MAP SHOWING THE CHIEF PLACES AND BATTLEFIELDS MENTIONED IN THE TEXT

GENERAL SURVEY

Centuries of peace have obliterated from the face of Britain the traces of past wars. Her coasts have been inviolate for nearly nine hundred years, no battle has taken place on her soil since 1746. Only today battles are fought in the sky above us more daring, desperate and skilful than any fought on our soil, and destruction undreamt of by Scottish riever or Cromwellian trooper, by Norman knight or baronial rebel, falls from the air.

We live, as a people, very much in the present: so much so that our history often seems as turf-grown as our battlefields. The local antiquarian remembers, sometimes the military historian visits the site, more occasionally the pious pilgrim. There was a faded bunch of heather tied with a tartan bow on the monument at Flodden when last I saw it. But streets of small houses transect the field at Turnham Green where the city trained bands blocked the Cavaliers' dash for London in 1642 and the trolley buses trundle across the place where Yorkist lines were drawn at Barnet in 1471.

It is a different Fleet Street today from the narrow cleft between out-jutting, half-timbered houses where Thomas Wyatt's rebel forces were trapped and cut down after forcing their way into London through Temple Bar one Spring day in 1554. But where the green field of Tewkesbury sleeps in the peaceful arm of the Severn, one patch of ground is called the Red Piece still, and at Chalgrove Field within the memory of man oral tradition among the older villagers remembered the young crops trampled down by Cavalier and Roundhead horse on June 18th 1643 when John Hampden was killed. 'Field was down to oats that year.'

Some battlefields of course are different. Hastings, Bannockburn, Dunbar, Marston Moor, Naseby have become fighting grounds for antiquaries and military historians; rivers of ink flow for rivers of blood. Tempers rise. Polite sarcasm becomes unabashed rudeness. None so ruthless as the antiquary on the warpath. Many of the disputes seem academic to the dispassionate observer, for who knows what really takes place in a battle. Certainly not the combatants: how then the historian? Something more and less than knowledge is needed, something without which knowledge is useless. The sense of the past, the imaginative mind which can think the scene again, call into being the fears and the 'hopes of the brief intensified hour, see that bend of the stream round the willow clump, this gentle dip, that bare hillock as the anxious soldier saw it, feel the sun or the mist of three centuries ago to be the sun and the mist of to-day, let the landscape teem suddenly with its long-buried dead, call up the blood of a hundred humble ancestors and send it racing through twentieth century veins.

See you our stilly woods of oak,
And the dread ditch beside?
O that was where the Saxons broke
On the day that Harold died.

See you the windy levels spread
About the gates of Rye?
O that was where the Norseman fled,
When Alfred's ships came by.'

Trite? Possibly: but how much they miss who lack this sense of place and heritage, who do not see in Malden estuary the tall black prows of the Danes, or in the Highland glen the crouching clansmen of Montrose? For in spite of many changes, the landscape as we know it meets us in many an ancient chronicle of war. The stunted thorn tree and the slippery, sheep-bitten slope of the hillside at Alfred's Battle of Ashdown; the 'foul narrow lanes' round Tewkesbury and the 'fair champaign country of Cotteswold' on the march thither; the 'hoar apple tree' and the chalky down at Hastings; the untidy wasteland with its gorse clumps at Marston Moor. The weather too is wonderfully familiar: fog at Barnet, a March snowstorm at Towton, a blustering wet August for King Charles's Cornish campaign in 1644, the soft Highland mists which blotted out Culloden and swathed Auldearn; the 'deluge of dropping showers,' at Dunbar; the occasional dazzling summer day – Naseby, fought on June 14th 1645, Killiecrankie on July 27th 1689.

The landscape of the past is preserved to us most strikingly in accounts of battles. At few other times did our ancestors (before the eighteenth century) think it worthy of description in detail. It may be these topographical and climatic stage directions which give to accounts of battles their extraordinary vividness. It may be that which leads some of us into the strange, fascinating, inexhaustible adventure of tracing them. Not as historians, not as antiquarians, but simply for love of the tantalising game, for the incidental pleasures of unknown country and odd encounters, the vicar with the unpublished monograph on the local skirmish, the ardent antiquary who can prove to you exactly where the Roman standard was placed, the prisoners' names scratched on the font, the playful bullocks which made Prince Maurice's brisk skirmish at Chewton Mendip so hard to concentrate on, the cool loveliness of the Yarrow in September on the track of Montrose to Philiphaugh, the neo-Gothic turret on the crest of Edgehill from which King Charles did not, but we may, admire the view. Who, that has not experienced it, knows the mounting excitement as the dead words of 'authorities' assume reality with the help of the ordnance map and the outspread view? Here then is the brook which foiled the cavalry, babbling over its stones as it has done these thousand years: think away the Georgian house on the left, and think back that plantation of trees which vanished two hundred years ago. Gradually the coherent picture emerges. Is it the same as Sir Charles Oman has given in the Art of War, or Macaulay, or John Buchan? Does it matter very much if it is not? You have lived the fearful hour again, and to re-live the past is the whole centre and secret of history. You have learnt something too of the uncertainties, the margin for error in the whole historical science, and are, maybe, the wiser for it.

The amateur of battles need not concern himself overmuch with the time before the Conquest. True that by far the most, and the bloodiest fighting took place in these earlier days, but its topography is vague, though Maiden Castle stands, a gigantic monument to the fortress architecture of the Neolithic age. Where Caesar landed, or Caratacus made his last stand we do not know for certain.

The great line of Roman forts from the Wash to Beachy Head were the strong points of organised Roman defence against the Saxon invader under that nobly named official, the Count of the Saxon Shore. These at least mark in impressive ruin an early strategic line. But where the outnumbered Britons won a rare victory against their Saxon conquerors by vociferously chanting 'Hallelujah' – odd foreshadowing of a Cromwellian technique – that we do not know.

The main strategic features of the dogged campaigning of Alfred and his successors against the Danes are clear, but the details are blurred, and the battle sites doubtful. From these earlier times generalisations only emerge. The vulnerability of the island in the south and east for instance, so that conquest sweeps usually from southeast to northwest across the island; the lack of really difficult country, really impregnable fastnesses except in the west and the north, so that the older peoples are driven back, time and again to the highlands of Wales and Scotland and Cumberland, where through the whole length of history the older language and the older religion, and the older loyalties linger on.

A few exceptions stand out; the last Saxon stand against the Normans was in the fen country and Alfred's place of refuge before his great comeback against the Danes was 'in great sorrow and unrest amid the woods and marshes of the land of Somerset.'

England itself lacks massive or forbidding features. The

Cheviots never presented any serious obstacle to invasion in either direction; the Romans had to defend the line with a wall on which they kept continual watch, and it was in mid-winter 1644 that David Leslie and five thousand troops crossed them, deep in snow. The real strategic barrier in the north was the long estuary and line of the Forth, a line which the Romans however failed to hold although they occupied it, but which recurs time and again as the pivot of internal Scottish wars. In the South, the Chilterns were to prove an effective barrier to attacks on London from Oxford in the Civil War, if only because their north-western face, turned towards the King's attacking forces, though not high, is exceptionally steep. Reading, in the only passable gap, changed hands repeatedly.

In Wales on the other hand the *massif* of Snowdonia forms a strong defence in front of the rich corn-growing lands of Carnarvon and Anglesea. Here in the thirteenth century Llewelyn ap Griffith was to defy English attack, until the wily Edward I with the help of his fleet came on the position from the rear. Scotland was to prove wholly impregnable from the south; not only did the long transverse slash of the Forth make a defensive line of extraordinary strength in front of the Highlands, but the distances by sea and the firm Scottish control of their own coasts made encirclement impossible, although more than once (by Protector Somerset in 1547, by Cromwell in 1651) an English fleet was brought up to the support of an English army. The battle of Pinkie in 1547 must indeed be one of the earliest examples of a combined operation. Stirling, commanding what was for centuries the only bridge over the Forth was the key to the entire

Scottish hinterland, and both in the internal wars of the Scots, and the wars with England, the storm centre of the fighting, from Wallace's victory at Cambuskenneth in 1298 to Sheriffmuir in 1715.

When invasion threatened, the lookouts along our indented coasts aroused the country by the flare of beacons. For the Spanish Armada and for the Napoleonic threat, the brushwood was piled up and the watchers ready on every signal height:

> 'Far on the deep the Spaniard saw, along each southern shire,
> Cape beyond cape, in endless range, those twinkling points of fire.'

Meanwhile, from the coast inland, in widening flashes, the signal leapt:

> 'Till the proud peak unfurl'd the Hag o'er Darwen's rocky dales,
> Till like volcanoes flared to Heaven the stormy hills of Wales,
> Till 'twelve fair counties saw the blaze on Malvern's lonely height.
> Till streamed in crimson on the wind the Wrekin's crest of light.'

A false alarm caused by an accidental fire in Northumberland set the beacons leaping across the lowlands of Scotland in Napoleon's time. The Borderers sprang to arms and marched to defend the coasts.

It was a time which Sir Walter Scott recollected 'with feelings which we can hardly hope to make the rising generation comprehend. Almost every individual was either enrolled in a military or civil capacity, for the purpose of contributing to resist the long suspended threats of invasion ...' Not so difficult for our rising generation to comprehend.

In Scotland too the symbol of the fiery cross, a flaming torch of heather carried by a runner, was the accepted means of mobilising the manhood of the clans against attack. We have mention of it before Pinkie and during Montrose's campaigns.

The castle plays a comparatively small part in English warfare, as the forethought of Kings prevented their nobles from making themselves independent in fortresses of their own. Not castles but quiet manor houses placed by chance in strategic positions, became in the time of Charles I the centre point of elaborate defence and systematic reduction; pretty Bletchindon near Oxford, spacious Basing in Hampshire, the charming Compton Winyates, the palatial residence of Lord Noel at Chipping Campden.

Latham and Pomfret, even, although genuine castles, were a couple of centuries out of date, Even less well prepared were Salcombe, Pendennis, and Portland in the west country, castles indeed, but built by Henry VIII with all their defences to the seaward side – against a foreign invasion which had not come. Their elderly and virgin guns were turned by the King's friends in 1643 against a landward enemy, and their ineffective rear walls hastily improved to meet a Contingency their architects had not foreseen.

Regular sieges to cities were few except in the Civil War. They were quick to open their gates in the earlier baronial contests, the citizens being never anxious to risk the danger of an assault or a sack. The difference in the seventeenth century conflict was that they were garrisoned, so that the decision for surrender or resistance no longer lay with the citizens. It was not to gratify the

Parliamentarian or Royalist sympathies of the people of Oxford or Colchester, York or Hull that these towns resisted their attackers. Poor Colchester indeed groaned for surrender, the people dying of hunger, the Parliamentarian guns raking the city from the hill above, while the Royalist garrison held grimly on. London was never closely invested, thanks to the Chiltern Ridge, and the strong defences pivoting on the battery at Hyde Park Corner were not put to the test.

Next in importance to the shape of the country, whether natural or artificial is the character of the people. Without venturing too far into the morass of racial characteristics, it is possible to distinguish certain persistent qualities and failings. The English – differing here from the Scots – were always reputed to be good shots, whether with bow and arrow, with musket or with rifle. 'The best shots in the world,' said Philippe de Commines in the fifteenth century, and when English archers under Coeur de Lion occupied Messina in 1190 we have an even odder tribute: 'no man could look out of doors but he would have an arrow in his eye before he could shut it.'

The unbroken square, the determined last stand has been characteristic of Scots and English alike, Celts and Saxons. Originally it seems to have been not so much a characteristic as the characteristic of Anglo-Saxon warfare. The warriors stood shield to shield and shoulder to shoulder round their Chieftain. An immobile wall of defence, the formation could not easily be converted for attack. The Saxon characteristic is a dogged determination; the Celtic a more desperate one, the hopeless heroism often found among outnumbered, overwhelmed, defeated peoples. Conservatism is a constant characteristic: Caesar found the Britons fighting from chariots, a difficult technique long abandoned even by the Gauls.

King Henry VIII at the Field of the Cloth of Gold paraded his company of bowmen proudly before the French King who had long since discarded such weapons, and more than a hundred years later the bow was used, on one occasion at least, in the time of Charles I. The pike has been extolled as late as 1940. The character of political institutions too is of importance in modifying methods of warfare. In England itself, from the middle ages onwards, the combatants competed for the approval of the civil population. In political warfare, whether for the succession of a dynasty, or the privileges of a class, it was always a part of the game to win over the opposing side and pacify the usually indifferent populace. The civilian indeed forms a recognisable third party.

Over the border in Scotland the tale is more gruesome, perhaps because a clash of races was involved; perhaps because religion played a more dynamic part, and religion is a great inspirer both of vindictiveness and propaganda; perhaps because the wars of Scotland continued longer and with fewer intervals than those of England. But above all because war was not, at least in the Highlands, confined to a recruited soldiery. The manhood of the clans rose en masse and the civilian 'third party' did not exist. This is an essay in one aspect of the past, an account of 'old, unhappy, far-off things, and battles long ago.' We are concerned only with recapturing men in action and the landscape of their time; of the motives behind the action, this is not the place to treat. Somehow unity came out of the warring races in Great Britain. The Saxon conquered the Celt, was conquered by the Norman; the older races, the older religions, the older loyalties perished, gave way and were absorbed into the new. There is no great cause for glorying in our internal broils. On that aspect of the matter a little sixteenth century clerk, writing after the battle of Pinkie has said the aptest word:'Not one of us all is any whit prouder of it, than would be the tooth that hath bit the tongue.'

HASTINGS

OCTOBER 14TH 1066

The battlefield of Hastings, marked to this day by the abbey which the grateful Conqueror erected as nearly as possible to the centre of the Saxon position, is one of those rare engagements which is not only historically but tactically significant. Both defending Saxons and invading Normans were well led, and the contest posed a problem which was to be the central problem of mediaeval warfare for three centuries.(The art of war was of slow development in those times.) Saxon tactics were strong in the defensive. They knew how to range themselves in the shield-wall, that is in a close circle, shield to shield. Armed with spears and short swords their method was first to throw their weapons at the enemy and, when they had sufficiently disorganised him; to break formation and go for their scattered opponents hand to hand with swords. The fighting, once the ring was broken, became a matter of individual prowess. The organised infantry charge was beyond Saxon training. Should the enemy take the initiative, the shield wall with its projecting spears could withstand the attack of equal forces almost indefinitely. Cavalry in large numbers was unknown in England.

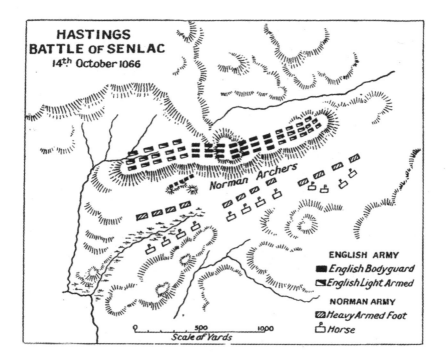

This was the innovation of Hastings, for William, undeterred by the problem of transport, brought over a contingent of mounted knights. He also brought a number of bowmen. The Saxons were thus to find themselves aced by an enemy infinitely more mobile than any they had met before, and armed with missiles which, if less individually damaging, were more continuously irritating than the fierce shower of spears which they had been taught both to deliver and to expect. Against an enemy whose equipment and tactics differed so much from their own, the Saxons' only hope lay in a clever exploitation of the ground. The situation, so far from being a freak, was one which was to recur whenever a poorer and more primitive people opposed a more highly organised and wealthier one, for cavalry is a matter of finance and of the social structure of society. At Hastings and in the five weeks which preceded it the unhappy Harold proved himself a soldier of resource and discretion, but his was a lost cause. In the first place the defenceless coasts of his kingdom (he had no navy) were assaulted in two places at once. He was in London, expecting daily the news of William's attack in the south, when on September 15th 1066 he received the unnerving intelligence that William's ally the King of Norway, had landed in the north, ravaged Scarborough and was threatening York. His mobile forces – a few thousands only – were too small to divide. Relying on the local *fyrd* (a kind of homeguard which would not fight outside its respective county) to watch the south coast, he marched rapidly north. On September 26th he met and defeated the Norwegians at Stamford Bridge. It had taken him less than a fortnight to make his way across nearly two hundred miles of broken, unroaded country, and to deal finally with his assailant. But on September 28th William of Normandy had landed at Pevensey with a considerable host of horse and foot. The *fyrd* had temporarily relaxed their watch for it was a holiday (the English weekend is an old institution), and the Norman troops disembarked without a blow given or received.

Harold, with his tired, victorious army was already hastening south. He knew of William's landing about October 2nd; by the 8th he was in London. As much a statesman as a soldier, William had made no attempt to rush the capital in Harold's absence, for he knew well that the citizens, who might close their gates while Harold was still King, would throw them open as soon as Harold was defeated. Better therefore to settle with his enemy in open country and enter the chief city as a welcomed conqueror than to antagonise its people by assault. So he waited on the coast. He had landed well out of reach of the small garrison and impressive fortress of Dover. Here was another strong point which would fall into his hand as soon as the Saxon King was conquered.

Had he been sure of William's quiescence, Harold might have given his standing army longer to recuperate or waited for a few reinforcements promised from some nobles of doubtful loyalty in the Midlands. But he could not be sure, and his intelligence service was belated and inadequate. He decided to take the initiative and that at once. He marched south and on the evening of October 13th sighted William's army from the crest of the South Downs.

Both from what he could see himself and from the reports of his scouts and the country folk, he must have realised that he had before him a very different task from the reduction of his last enemy. There, he had been fighting on an equality and in a manner he understood. Now he had to meet not only superior numbers but the problem of cavalry.

William was however in the lower ground and it was possible for Harold in the falling dusk to choose an admirable defensive position. High on a forward spur of the down grew a 'hoar apple tree,' and here Harold set his standard. He ranged his troops – their numbers are not easy to estimate, but they can hardly have been more than seven thousand, and perhaps only half that number – on the brow of the down where the ground at their backs sloped very steeply away. An isthmus of land connected this hill with the broader downs behind, but this isthmus in Harold's time was sparsely wooded and behind it the further down was covered in forest. Thus, if the shield-wall of the Saxons should break under the Norman pressure, the army could scatter down the precipitous slopes and take refuge in the woods where no cavalry could pursue. Harold hoped, doubtless, that William's men would exhaust themselves in repeated vain, uphill charges, be at length demoralised by the hurling of spears among their masses, and so yield, as Danes and feebler Saxons had yielded before, to the scattered vindictive attack of his swordsmen when at last they broke their ring and advanced.

The terrible day of October 14th 1066 proved both the courage of Harold's troops and the wisdom of their leader. How long the battle lasted we cannot know, but every chronicle and legend, every ballad and romance tell of its intensity and stubborn length. Almost from sunrise, almost to sunset of an October day: it is a long time. William's cavalry charging with the ground against them, were thrown back more than once by the Saxon spearmen. But they were not a primitive people, easily disordered. They could withdraw as well as advance, reform and charge again. Saxon missiles must ultimately give out, Saxon nerves fail. Moreover, and more serious, the retreating foe was a temptation to Harold's men to break their ranks and follow. They were not drilled to act perpetually in formation; they were individual warriors, reckless and proud, who were used to boasting, over their mead bowls after the conflict, how many they had slain. In twos and threes they broke from the shield wall, tore down the slope after the retreating Normans, left the once-solid phalanx round the hoar apple-tree gashed and ragged.

Later writers, poets and historians, have regulated these individual exhibitions of Saxon prowess. They have declared that William ordered a feigned retreat and drew the Saxons after him in one fatal charge. But feigned retreat, at least at such close quarters as those of Hastings, would seem to be one of those manoeuvres invented by civilians. Psychologically and physically it would have needed a degree of training and self-control beyond even the prowess of the Normans. Nor was it necessary.

As Harold's position was gradually weakened by the rashness of his own men, William intensified the attack of his bowmen. They were not generally regarded as a very important branch of his troops, nor were there very many of them. A few hundreds, perhaps. The Bayeux tapestry shows them, lightly armed, carrying a quiver of small arrows and the childish-looking little bows, not a yard long, which they hold before their faces and draw back to their noses, no further. The light projectiles of sharpened wood probably tipped with steel had to be fired upwards at an absurdly high trajectory. Accurate aiming was impossible. The best the bowmen could do was to accompany the massed charge of the horse with a light, vicious shower into the centre of Harold's ranks. In the early stages of the battle it is difficult to believe that the Saxons, used to a hurricane of thrown spears, suffered much inconvenience from the noisy pattering of the Norman arrows. But some damage was done and undoubtedly the continuous irritation wore down Saxon patience and played its part in stinging the warriors to break their lines and set upon the foe.

The truth about Hastings is in all respects odder and sadder than the romantic fictions which from the earliest times have crowded round it. William, it is said, tired of Saxon stone-walling, commanded his bowmen to fire their arrows high into the air, and one of them thus struck the Saxon King in the eye. But William would not have needed to give any such order for no Norman bowman can have been losing off his arrows in any other way, and it was an extraordinary fluke of history that one of these feeble little shafts whistled home to its deadly target just as King Harold flung back his head. One second more, one second less and it had glanced off his helmet, scarcely felt.

The King's death settled the succession of England, and assured William's triumph. But the Saxons had their heroic tradition. It did not end the battle. That was only ended by the final Norman onslaught on the broken shield-wall. Some warriors escaped as Harold planned they should, down the slippery chalk slopes, back into the tangled wood. The greater number closed in round the hoar apple tree and their King's forlorn standard, and there were trampled down. The Norman knight rode over the Saxon foot soldier at Hastings, as for generations to come his descendants were to ride over their Saxon serfs.

THE WELSH WARS

1277-1295

FALKIRK

JULY 22ND 1298

BANNOCKBURN

JUNE 24TH 1314

D uring the next two centuries the English assimilated gradually with their conquerors and acquired under their guidance considerable proficiency in the technique of feudal warfare. The next group of battles worthy of attention begins in Wales in 1277 and ends at Bannockburn a generation later. Here, in conflicts between the now normanised English and their primitive neighbours, the Hastings problem is posed again: by what means can foot soldiers armed with spears overcome cavalry and bowmen? Only by evading and drawing on the enemy into unknown and difficult country could the Welsh and Scottish leaders, with their unmounted spearmen, occasionally bring disaster to the heavy-armed knights and trained archers of their attackers.

Since Hastings two changes had occurred in the feudal army. The cavalry composed of knights and horses ever more completely sheathed in steel, had grown more deadly in frontal attack, but far less mobile. Skirmishing was impossible; the 'charge' was delivered at a trot, but the impact was terrific. Speed and mobility had been completely sacrificed to weight. A feudal knight was more like one of our early tanks than our idea of a cavalryman.

The short bow too, had been replaced abroad by the mechanical crossbow, but in England by the un-mechanical longbow. Of 'wild elm, unpolished, rude and uncouth,' the longbow properly handled was exceptionally deadly. Its iron-tipped arrows had been known to pin an armed knight to his horse, piercing chain-mail, thigh and wooden saddle. It did not get out of order so easily as the crossbow, its aim was truer, and its shafts could be concentrated in a more rapid shower. 'Longbow and cavalry were, however, alike useless against an enemy who would not be drawn, and the Welsh Chieftain Llewelyn long defied King Edward I from his impregnable mountains. The climate was another powerful Welsh ally.

'Grevouse est la guerre, et dure a l'endurer;
Quand ailleurs est l'été, en Galles est hiver,'

complained a Norman rhymer, and not for some years could Edward induce his knights to prolong their campaigning into the bitter winter. This innovation proved the end of Llewelyn ap Grffith, who was at length forced to come out of hungry Snowdon to forage. His spearmen, caught and outflanked in the angle of the Wye and the Yrfon on December 11th 1282 succumbed like Harold's at Hastings to the joint attack of bowmen and cavalry.

Thirteen years later when renewed revolt brought Edward again to Wales, the Welsh spearmen found a better way of resisting the onslaught of the English knights. This time, as a chronicler relates, they 'fixed the butt ends of their spears in the ground and turned their points against the charging enemy.' The formidable hedgehog repulsed the first English charge. The snobbishness which existed between horse and foot still often misled the proud knights into imagining they could dispense with the help of their bowmen. Made wiser by their failure, the English advanced a second time with archers interspersed between their knights and this time destroyed the hedgehog from within by a hail of arrows. The tactics used by the Welsh in 1296 were used almost successfully three years later by William Wallace at Falkirk. The heroic lowlander, about whom the Scots resistance to Edward I had crystallised, had with a few thousand guerilla troops made himself master of the lowlands, totally defeated one of Edward's lieutenants with a lumbering force of cavalry at Stirling Bridge in September 1297, and even invaded England.

Edward I could hardly allow this state of affairs to continue, but the size of the army with which he set out for the North is sufficient tribute to what Wallace had done for the wilting spirit of Scotland. Edward seems to have had upwards of ten thousand foot and about two thousand horse when he crossed the Scots border in the following summer. Wallace made himself scarce. He lay low in the forest of Torwood between Falkirk and Stirling. The English would not venture in; he would not venture out. The size of the English army began to tell against it in the sparsely populated moorlands; Edward decided to withdraw.

This was Wallace's chance, now he would come out and fall on the English rear as they marched away. But his plan was betrayed, and Edward swung round and marched back to meet him. 'He shall not come to me, for I will go to him,' he said. On the way at Linlithgow his horse shied, threw him and broke two of his ribs. Undeterred he pushed on and came up at length with Wallace two miles south of Falkirk on July 22nd 1298.

Wallace had drawn up his spearmen – perhaps ten thousand in all, for his numbers had swollen with his success, in four masses, 'schiltrons' as they were called, their spearbutts in the ground, the front rank kneeling, so that any English knight who had been in Wales three years before would have recognised again the formidable hedgehog. This time there were four hedgehogs with handfuls of archers on the flanks and about two hundred horsemen in the rear. The whole of Wallace's front was protected by the bog called Darnrig Moss.

Edward's knights were formed into three battles, of which the centre, apparently without waiting for further orders, immediately attempted a frontal attack on Wallace's position. The heavy armed knights on their armoured horses floundered forward into the bog and there stuck. Those on the left, perceiving the bog, made a wide detour and formed for an attack on Wallace's right flank. All these movements were unhindered, for the Scots bowmen were

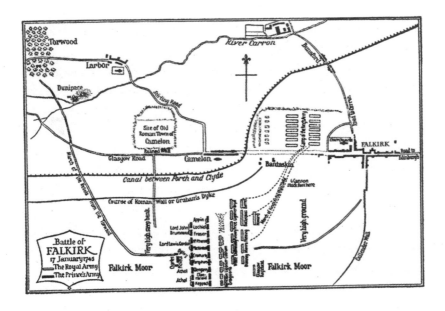

not numerous enough to harass them with fire, and were saving their arrows. Even the bogged knights managed to drag themselves clear without molestation, sweep out avoiding the bog on the further side and threaten Wallace's other flank. But at this point the knights made their usual mistake. It was extraordinary how little they had learnt by Welsh experience. Only the intelligent Bishop of Durham on the left wing attempted to moderate their enthusiasm, urging them not to charge the Scots before their own bowmen came up and prepared the way for them.

'Go and read your mass,' bellowed Ralph Basset, one of his knights, 'and don't teach us the art of war.' Unteachable indeed, he and his fellows trotted ponderously up the hill and were flung back on the bristling wall of spears. The same thing happened on the further side of the field to the contingent who had dragged themselves out of the bog.

It was true that Wallace's handful of cavalry and loose groups of archers had fled in terror before this double onset, but the schiltrons stood unbroken. A second charge as desperate as the first, and the remnants of the English knights would have limped back scattered and weary, an easy prey to the Scottish spearmen. But at this moment Edward himself came up with his main army and the infantry. While the knights re-formed, the bowmen were brought forward and ordered to aim at fixed points in the Scottish ranks. Wallace had neither defence nor answer, within a few moments the great schiltrons showed irregular gashes. The dead and wounded, falling among the twelve foot spears, put their 'comrades' into disorder. Closing up was difficult, after a little while impossible. It remained only for the English knights to concentrate their charge on the weakest points in the wavering wall of spears to break the schiltrons open. Wallace himself got off the field alive into the woods at his back, but his army was shattered, and of those who escaped the shambles at the hilltop many were drowned swimming across the river Carron in headlong flight for the north.

The defeat of Falkirk had come within sight of being a victory. The colossal stubbornness of the "schiltrons" had proved a match for a massed cavalry charge far more violent than anything which had been seen in Wales; the formation tried out by the Welsh and perfected by Wallace was to be the basic method of infantry fighting up to the seventeenth century, outlasting the heavy armed cavalry and long surviving the introduction of firearms.

The task of uniting and liberating the Scottish Kingdom was to be accomplished during the next generation by Robert Bruce. He recognised the limitations of the forces at his command and for long enough took to the hills, harassing the English where and how he could. His tactics are best described in the rhyming lines of his so-called testament, the admirable advice which he left to his subjects and which they put into practice in the Highlands for the next four centuries.

> On fut suld be all Scottis weare,
> By hyll and mosse themselff to reare, Lat woods for walls be bow and speare That enemies
> do them na deire.
> In strait places gar keep all store,
> And burn the plainland them before.
> With wiles and wakings of the night And mickle noise made on height
> Them shall ye turn with great aifray
> As they were chased with sword away.

Scorched earth, swift surprise, the terror which a few men scattered in the trackless bracken, hidden in the unknown glen, can bring to a great host: so Montrose will master all Scotland with his two thousand 'wild Hieland men'; so the heather will stir, whisper and come alive at Killiecrankie.

But one pitched battle Robert Bruce gave the English, the only one in recorded mediaeval history in which infantry totally and overwhelmingly defeated cavalry. The battle of Bannockburn, fought on June 24th 1314, trails such a cloud of legend that it is difficult now to disentangle what actually took place, still more, where it took place. Much ink has been spilled, many antiquaries' tempers lost over the true acreage which, within the angle of

Bannockburn and the river Forth, just to the southeast of Stirling in the parish of St. Ninian's, is the actual site of the great contest. The details of the battle are no less blurred. Authority now seems to repudiate that romantic story that Bruce's camp followers, waving sheets and fragments of coloured linen, suddenly appeared round what is still called Gillies' hill, and panicked the English forces who mistook them for a powerful reinforcement.

What remains, however, is still a remarkable story, the defeat of an army of twenty thousand, of which over three thousand were cavalry, by a force of less than seven thousand, almost all on foot. When in the summer of 1314 King Edward II, the vacillating son of a tremendous father, invaded Scotland, Bruce withdrew to the Forth, knowing that Edward would tire his troops and strain his commissariat in crossing the wasted lands to the south.

The English objective was the relief of Stirling Castle commanding the only bridge over the river, which, by an arrangement common in mediaeval warfare, the defenders had agreed to surrender on midsummer's day, if no relief came. On June 23rd 1314, Edward's huge and already tired army was within sight of the fortress. Bruce, holding the main road to the castle, had pitted it with pot-holes extending right across the only stretch of open land. Woods and copses formed additional defence. After a preliminary attempt Edward's advance guards gave it up.

They had suffered a distressing shock, when one of their steel clad knights, de Bohun, had thundered down on the Scots King as he trotted in front of his own line mounted on a light pony. De Bohun relied on weight, but Bruce's nimble steed swerved neatly, and as the massive knight hurtled past, the Scots King felled him

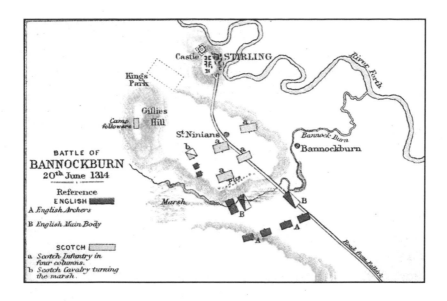

with a single blow of his battleaxe. It was a bad omen.

Baffled, the English now decided to outflank Bruce by following the course of the little river Bannock which joins the Forth a few miles below Stirling, cross it in the marshy flats near its confluence with the Forth and thus fall on Bruce's flank. The ground here was, however, marshy and very difficult for heavy cavalry, while on the drier and higher ground above the Scots were drawn up. Should Bruce attack, the English would have no room to manoeuvre with the Bannock so close at their backs. Edward's whole plan was based on the belief that spearrnen would never take the initiative against cavalry; he was counting on Falkirk all over again.

The sun rises early on midsummer's day in Scotland. The first streak of daylight found the English host very uncomfortably huddled on the marshy flat in the angle of the Bannock and the

Forth. Their main body was across the stream, but had not yet formed up for battle. Bruce gave it no time to do so. He saw that this was the one occasion in a thousand when his pikemen could be more than a match for Edward's cavalry. To their dismay the English suddenly saw in the white light of the early morning, the phalanxes of spears come formidably into motion. The 'schiltrons' hurled themselves on the floundering English cavalry.

It was by no means an easy victory. For a long time the huge masses of horse and foot stood locked together but the English cavalry desperately trying to extricate itself, had not sufficient room to draw out and charge again. The only hope was the bowmen; but the infantry was still in the rear, and not properly drawn up. Flights of arrows discharged over the heads of their own troops did a little damage to the Scots but far more to the struggling English horse. When some of the archers at last managed to outflank their own cavalry and direct a swift, deadly fire into the Scottish schiltrons, Bruce was ready for them, with a small contingent of light, mobile horsemen, the only cavalry he possessed. These now charged in to ride the English bowmen down. With their dispersal the last hope of the English was gone. Those that had not fallen on the Scottish pikes fled in disorder.

Collapse was absolute: it was, declares Sir Charles Oman, 'the most lamentable defeat which an English army ever suffered.' It is a reassuring thought for the people of a now united Britain that they suffered it at the hands of the Scots.

BARNET

APRIL 14TH 1471

TEWKESBURY

MAY 5TH 1471

BOSWORTH

AUGUST 22ND 1485

Two and a half centuries divide Bannockburn from the Wars of the Roses, and the gentle neurotic Edward II from the tough young hearty Edward IV. Three hundred miles divide the marsh and woods and crags of the Forth from the homely landscape of Barnet and the wide green flats of Severnside at Tewkesbury. The art of war too had altered. The longbow was disappearing before the crossbow. Gunpowder had been invented. Cannon were in occasional use. The heavy armed knight had grown heavier and heavier until he had, almost literally, sunk into the ground. At Agincourt the French knights, in plate from head to foot, had stuck hock deep in the mud and broken their horses' legs trying to get out. Elderly knights died of heart failure under the weight of their armour. Mild casualties suffocated before their friends could stand them upright and crack open their battered shells.

By the time that Edward IV was King of England, the aristocracy had a new technique of fighting. They used their horses for transport, but dismounted when the fighting began.

Of the many campaigns between Yorkists and Lancastrians, that of 1471 which ended in the Battle of Tewkesbury is the only one in which an interesting strategy is discernible. From an entire generation of intermittent fighting the Wars of the Roses cast up no outstanding military figure. Edward IV who was cool, daring and an efficient strategist stands out among a crowd of nonentities. The winter of 1470-1 found him an exile in Flanders, having been unceremoniously tumbled out of his Kingdom by the Earl of Warwick, who had again set up the feeble-minded Henry VI and re-called Henry's energetic wife Margaret of Anjou and her son from France.

In March 1471 Edward sailed from Flushing for England with about 1200 men. Of these three hundred were Flemish professionals armed mysteriously with 'hand guns' – probably an improved crossbow fired by a charge of powder. He found East Anglia manned against him, and with astonishing daring continued up the coast and landed at Ravenspur in the estuary of the Humber, choosing the place for the bold reason that the country, being notoriously hostile to him, would not have been garrisoned against him. Years of war had taught country folk to interfere as little as possible with armies, and hostile civilians, Edward rightly judged, might not welcome, but would not stop him.

The next problem was to reach London, with two Lancastrian armies across his path. He had far too weak a force to risk a battle; lightning speed and dexterity in evading his enemies was his only hope. He slid round the first Lancastrian army at Tadcaster by way of Wakefield and Doncaster, and threw himself into Nottingham to regain breath. It was March 23rd 1471, a week since his landing. But his position was acutely dangerous, for he now had hostile armies behind at Tadcaster and before, at Coventry, while a third was approaching from East Anglia by way of Newark. This was the smallest, and Edward by marching straight out to meet it, bluffed its general into a hasty retreat to Lincolnshire. He kept up the pretence of pursuit only until his enemy was moving briskly backwards, then turned in his tracks and reached Leicester on March 27th. This at last was friendly country and the local magnates joined him with their bands of retainers.

The army in his rear had now completely lost track of his movements and was panting two days march behind. There was still Warwick himself at Coventry, but he was nervous of fighting Edward's swollen forces and stupidly let him slip past, to be joined by fresh sympathisers at Banbury on April 3rd. Hence he had a clear road to London, which he entered in triumph a week later.

Forty-eight hours was all Edward had in London, for Warwick with the three Lancastrian armies united was now in motion. On April 3rd, marching down the great North Road, Warwick camped at Monken Hadley, a mile north of Barnet. Edward came out to the defence of his newly regained capital and lay the same night

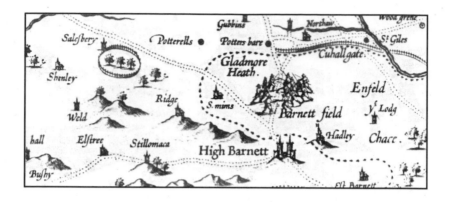

just north of Barnet and only a little distance from the place where today the unending suburbs of Greater London drop away with such astounding suddenness into a country almost as green as the country Edward saw.

Not, in fact, that Edward saw it that day, for the morning of April 14th, 1471 rose in dense fog. All the previous night had been pointlessly busy, for both sides had fired intermittently towards the spot where they took the other to be. Both had fired wide. The whole battle was indeed a series of groping miscalculations. With daylight, or a little earlier, for one account says specifically at four in the morning, the two armies felt towards each other blindly, and the front lines locked unevenly, each unintentionally out flanking the other's left wing. The outflanked Yorkist wing fled in disorder; the outflanked Lancastrian wing maintained its order though losing ground. In the centre the light was even, and probably the loss of the Yorkist left would have brought final disaster to Edward had not an extraordinary chance demoralised the Lancastrians. Their right wing, after its successful defeat of the Yorkist left, had been reassembled by its commander, Lord Oxford, with the intention of attacking Edward from the rear. In the mist Oxford and his men completely lost their bearings. One damp field looked exactly like another. They could hear the direction of the battle: that was all.

Suddenly, they loomed out of the mist not on the Yorkist rear, but in the rear of their fellow Lancastrians. It need not have mattered, but in the gloom the Lancastrians took the star on Oxford's banner for the Sun in Splendour which was Edward's device, and greeted the returning troops with a shower of arrows. They in their turn assumed that they had fallen among traitors - changing sides on the field of battle was not unknown in the Wars of the Roses - and set up a cry of 'Treason' which finally demoralised the Lancastrian left, who 'fled in disorder.

'This battayle duryd,' said a chronicler, 'fightynge and skirmishing, ryght doubtefully, because of the myste, by the space of three hours, ere it was fully achivyd.' It was fully achieved by the time the Lancastrian left broke. Warwick who was old-fashioned enough usually to fight mounted so as to oversee his men, had adopted the modern fashion on this occasion, so as not to appear inferior to the young giant Edward swinging his sword valorously and on foot in the forefront of his own line. He lived to regret the decision, but only just. Running to Wrotham Park where he had left his horse 'one came upon him and killed him and despoiled him naked.' So died the Kingmaker, the greatest and meanest trouble-maker in the history of England.

Edward IV had barely disbanded his army and settled down to enjoy his regained kingdom – he was a monarch who knew how to

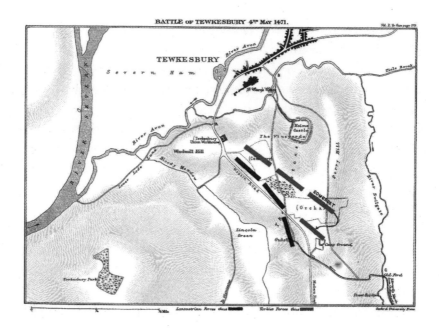

BATTLE OF TEWKESBURY 4ᵀᴴ MAY 1471.

enjoy himself – when he heard to his dismay that Margaret of Anjou, undeterred by the annihilation of her ally, had landed at Weymouth and was advancing inland. Exasperated, Edward reassembled his dispersed forces – about three thousand men – and headed for Cirencester, the junction of all the Roman roads in the west and therefore the likeliest place to cut her off. She turned towards Gloucester, meaning to join with friends in Wales, but Gloucester, with phenomenal loyalty for a fifteenth century city, refused to let her in. Edward meanwhile, after a thirty mile forced march over the top of the Cotswolds on one of the hottest and thirstiest days in the year, came up with her at Tewkesbury. Here, Margaret made her stand, the Severn and the Swillgate brook at her back and the abbey beyond, and in front muddy ditches and straggling hedgerows. This was well enough until Edward's forces carried the ditch and outflanked the position. At this point an altercation between two of Margaret's generals ended in one braining the other with his battle axe, whereupon defeat became total rout.

The Battle of Bosworth in 1485 with which the Wars of the Roses ended is of more dramatic than military interest, an example to daunt tyrants. Richard III brought more than three times the strength of his opponent, Henry Tudor, into the field. But when he gave the order to advance, one half of his army refused to budge and the other half walked with open arms to greet the opposing forces. The hag-ridden Richard of legend sought to escape crying

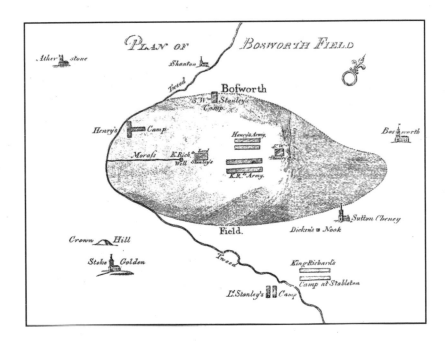

'A horse, a horse, my kingdom for a horse'; it seems more likely that the historical Richard saw death coming and went to meet it, grimly determined to die a King. He was wearing his crown, a gesture as dramatic as it was unusual. There was nothing half-hearted in the character of Richard Crookback. Bosworth lies in the heart of England among the thick-spread prosperous villages, the rolling country and the checkered hedgerows of the shires which were to see, a century and a half later, the defeat of King by Parliament on Naseby field. Undisturbed by internal wars in the long interval, England experienced invasion only from her Scottish neighbours.

FLODDEN

September 9th 1513

Flodden is certainly one of the noblest as it is one of the most interesting sites this side of the border. The bare, impressive slope, the quiet fields sloping to the Till, the line of the river, partly seen and partly hidden from the eminence of Flodden Edge, have an air of immemorial peace. Only the small monument with its brief line 'To the Brave of Both Nations' recalls that here on September 9th 1513 King James IV and all his chivalry perished. He had invaded England in mid-August with the – for that time – enormous army of forty thousand men, well furnished with the newest artillery of the clay. The veteran Earl of Surrey, over seventy and travelling mostly by coach on account of his rheumatism, was sent against him with as large an army as could hastily be gathered, chiefly from the northern counties. He had between twenty and twenty-six thousand men.

James had taken up on the steep brow of Flodden Edge, in the angle between the Till and its small tributary the Glen, a defensive position so strong that no sane foe would dare to attack. The formidable position was, in the long run, a weakness, for James was strong enough for a pitched battle and in fact wanted one.

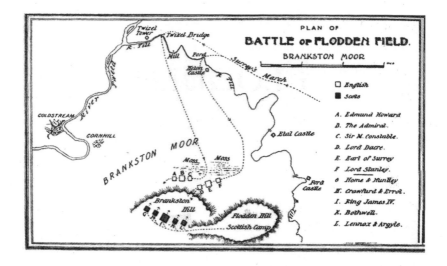

But Surrey would not attack him where he was and preferred to take the risk of circumventing the position and trying to draw the Scots from it. Immediately behind Flodden Edge, and separated from it by a shallow dip, stretches the broad summit of Branxton Hill.

Surrey's plan was to march up the hill, putting half his army across at Sandyford and the rest half a mile beyond at Twizel Bridge, and so, if possible, surprise the Scots from the rear by seizing Branxton Hill. It was, to say the least of it, a risky manoeuvre, for the route was in great part overlooked from the east end of Flodden Edge, and it was more than likely that King James would fall on the English army while it was crossing the river in two separate bodies.

Why he did not do so is, and will always be, doubtful. Not, presumably, out of any misguided chivalry; more probably because he had reckoned on a pitched battle and doubted his and his officers' ability to keep control of their forces if they forsook the high ground and delivered a long-distance attack on the English at the river. Instead, when he saw what Surrey was doing, James merely reversed his order of battle. His army had been drawn up on Flodden Edge, facing south. Now he moved it back to Branxton Hill itself, and turned its face north. With forty thousand men, the operation was difficult, and the new position less defensible than the first; nevertheless he still had the advantage of the ground, and moreover the fires lighted by his camp followers to consume the rubbish behind them sent a heavy trail of smoke over the brow of Branxton Hill and hid the new dispositions from the English. The smoke screen was the effect of accident, not design, but it served a useful purpose.

Meanwhile Surrey's son, leading the van, was over Twizel bridge, but badly bogged by a marshy little brook, the Broxburn on the lower slopes of Branxton Hill, while Surrey himself was still fording the Till with the rearguard at Sandyford. This was the moment at which the Scots King chose to attack. Surrey receiving a frantic message from his son, barely got his forces over the ford and joined the two halves of his army before the Scottish charge could split the English host irrevocably in two.

The English right wing was in fact partly routed, but the victorious Scots, borderers for the most part, had no further idea of fighting. In a border foray, after routing one's opponents, no more was expected, and they did not grasp that Flodden was no ordinary foray. 'We have fought and won; let the rest do their part as well as we.' They replied to the Earl of Huntly who vainly tried to marshall them. Even so the Scots main body, though their charge was held by Surrey, might have won the day. Their initial impetus had been very great, carrying their pikemen far into the English lines, and their numbers were larger. Moreover they were bearing downhill, the English up. But their twelve-foot pikes proved very unhandy at close quarters, the English halberds cut and broke them down. Moreover James and his nobility followed the ancient practice of leading their troops in person. The English commanders, on this occasion at least, foreshadowed the tactics of the Duke of Plaza Toro. It was as well for them, because in the hand-to-hand fighting after the armies locked, the Scots lords and the Scots King fell at the outset, and their troops could not prevail with no one left to lead them.

So the evening found the Scots army dispersed, and five thousand dead on the northern slope of Branxton Hill, King James among them, his head, woefully shattered by a halberd stroke, at the furthermost place to which the Scottish charge had cleft the English ranks. He had died as he had lived, the leader of his people.

The greatest of the Stewart sovereigns, and during his lifetime the most beloved, James IV still ranks a long way behind his grand-daughter in Scottish legend. It is indeed chiefly for the sake of Mary Queen of Scots that the name of Carberry Hill evokes any echo. It was not in point of fact a battle – less even than Langside where her forces were finally dispersed. The insurgents against her made a brave show of war, with their massed regiments of pikemen, their huge, banners and their guns; and the show was enough. The French ambassador, who had last seen Mary as the elegant and beloved young Queen of France, now found her driven from her capital, clad in scarlet petticoat kilted to the knee, like any ballad heroine, but not so gay. Her own troops would not fight; Bothwell, superb as a lover, was no choice for a King. He had no alternative but to escape, and Mary (after her three weeks honeymoon) to surrender to her insurgent nobles.

Edgehill

October 23rd 1642

Marston Moor

July 2nd 1644

Europe had seen many changes in the art of war between Flodden and the Civil Wars of Charles I. Firearms had improved conspicuously; heavy artillery had become an important part of every army; cavalry had returned to fashion after the long predominance of infantry, and the rnusket was fulfilling much the same function, though in more deadly fashion, as the bow had done in the middle ages. Yet the lines of the seventeenth century battle fronts are but a little farther apart than those of the mediaeval and renaissance contests. Neither cannon nor musket carried much farther than the long bow and the tactics of infantry defence, with pikes, had hardly changed since the 'schiltrons' of Wallace and Bruce.

Edgehill remains easily the loveliest battle site in England. It should be seen near to the anniversary of the fighting – October

23rd – with its battlement of autumnal trees crowning the steep green slope, and spread out below it the wide Warwickshire landscape, distance on distance, with the great solitary trees in the hedgerows and the tall belts of woodland and the sleeping villages.

Alas for the vivid picture – so tempting to the romantic – of autumn sunlight on banners and breastplates and the shining flanks of horses, bred for the hunting field and new to the noise of war. It was in fact a dull day, and the summer had been wet and cold. Prince Rupert had recently broken his collar bone when his horse slipped on a sheet of ice, and the King's standard had collapsed ingloriously in the mud and drizzle when it had been raised at Nottingham on August 22nd.

King Charles had left notoriously disloyal London and after recruiting in the North and Western Midlands he was now marching for his capital with an army of five thousand horse, and ten thousand foot. The command was divided. An inexperienced cavalry officer of twenty-two, the King's nephew Rupert, Lieutenant General of the Horse, was in fact the moving spirit of the army.

The Parliamentary forces were larger. They numbered six thousand horse and twelve thousand foot, and their wholly undistinguished commander was the Earl of Essex, who had learnt all the rules of orthodox warfare and nothing whatever else in the Low Countries.

When the royal army, setting out from Worcester, made towards London, Essex came lumbering along behind it. Rupert, quickly seeing the advantage of the land, seized the sharp escarpment of Edgehill, five miles south of Warwick, and swung round to face his pursuer. The armies thus confronted each other on the night of October 22nd. On the following morning Rupert brought his cavalry down off the precipitous crest of the hill to the place where the trees now end and the gradient of the hillside becomes practicable.

The two armies were ranged in the conventional alignment of their time; cavalry on the wings, foot in the centre with a couple of cannon in between. The hill runs steeply down about three hundred yards to the hamlet of Radway round its little church; (a Royalist infantryman named Kingsmill has a monument there today – one of the many in the King's red uniform who were not to leave the field alive.) Beyond Radway the ground rises again but much less steeply, and here lay the Parliamentary army, their right flanked by a steep hedged lane, inexpressibly muddy, which ran straight up the face of the hill, and thus also covered the Royalist position on the left. Rupert, on the Royalist right, had ample elbow room; his subordinate Wilmot on the left was cramped, but also to some extent sheltered, by the hedges.

Rupert opened the battle, using a technique which dumbfounded Essex and was in fact completely new. When cavalry had come into fashion again in the sixteenth century there had evolved the extraordinary technique known as the 'caracole'. Trotting up to the enemy at a brisk but not overwhelming speed, the first line would halt within firing distance, let off their pistols, turn and trot back to their own rear. The second line would repeat the operation and so on. The armies did not join. This extraordinary *pas de deux* between opposing cavalry had gradually given place to a more violent technique; the front line would halt and fire as before, and then charge on into the opposing ranks and fight it out hand to hand with swords. This was the orthodox technique Essex had seen in action and Rupert had learnt in books. But in blissfully peaceful England the shortage of firearms meant that Rupert's hastily recruited cavalry were very scantily equipped. Shock was all they would have to rely on, and shock would not be achieved if they halted in the approved style. He drew them up therefore very close together, and briefly explained what he wanted them to do; no less than to hurl themselves in a compact mass at the cavalry ranged below them. They were to keep as close together as possible, to ride straight on and those that had firearms were not to use them until they were already engaged with the enemy.

These instructions seem to have, been given only a few minutes

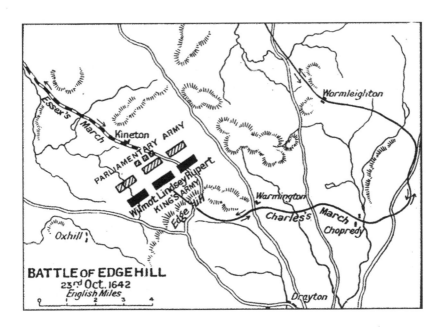

before the actual order to charge – time enough to let them sink in, but no longer, lest they be forgotten. Down smashed Rupert's cavalry and engaged Essex's panic stricken front. Had the Parliamentarians been prepared and well drilled they might have stood against the onslaught and the charge would have been held for a time at least in a series of separate duels all along the line. But Rupert's shock tactics were also surprise tactics. Amazement and impact together were too much. Essex's troops, as raw as Rupert's, broke in panic.

Now followed the really difficult operation for the victor, that of drawing together the excited pursuers and bringing them back to the help of their comrades on the hill. In this Rupert failed. His officers were few of them professionals who knew their job and most of them, like the men, were overheated with the preliminary triumph. Pursuit seemed natural to them, and off they went. It must have been more than an hour before their young general had again got together a large enough body to return to the King's main battle.

Here things had not gone too well. The Royalist left had become heavily entangled with the Parliamentary right on the muddier slopes and among the hedges on their side of the field, and though they had ultimately gained the advantage they were tired and dispirited. The real decision as so often with the seventeenth century battle, lay with the infantry in the centre. It was for them to hold the position while the cavalry did its swifter work on the wings. In vain to sweep your opponent's horse off the field if your own centre caved in behind you.

The King's infantry outnumbered and outgunned by Essex's

had put up a terrific stand. They had the better ground and, like Wallace's squares at Falkirk or Harold's at Hastings, stood immovable while Essex's line came for them in a hail of musketry fire. The hand to hand contest was exceptionally stubborn and the losses on the King's side heavy, his standard bearer being killed and the standard itself taken.

Rupert's return forced the Parliamentary infantry to withdraw and, with the evening fast drawing in, he sought his fellow commanders to get their consent to a final attack on the opposing army. Its left wing gone, its centre worn out and in some disorder, its right wing exhausted by the struggle in the lanes, it would be an easy prey for a joint attack from the Royalist cavalry. But he found no support. His fellow commanders were tired and probably resentful; here was this boy of twenty-two who had had an easy day on his side of the field, demanding fresh efforts of those who had made enough already. They called off the unfinished fight.

The King himself was sufficiently gratified by the recapture of his standard, by a bold young subaltern John Smith, who had ridden right through the enemy lines pretending to be a Parliamentarian, found the standard in Essex's tent and coolly carried it off on the pretence that Essex had sent for it, a feat for which he was very properly knighted in the field of battle.

It was King Charles's mistake never to give his finest soldier a free hand. After Edgehill, caution and political considerations prevented the swift march to London which Rupert fiercely counselled. Not two years later, when the active Prince had brilliantly relieved York, an inept message of recall from the King forced him to cut short his campaign and risk everything on an immediate battle. The forces of the Parliamentarians and the Scots (their allies) were about double those of Rupert. The general in command was the highly efficient Fairfax, under him a cavalry officer of rising reputation named Cromwell. It was this Cromwell, or rather the left wing which he commanded, which utterly defeated Rupert's cavalry in the battle fought just outside York at Marston Moor on July 2nd 1644.

This tragic and perplexed engagement is too complicated to admit of compression; it can only be fully understood on the field itself where recently a monument has been set up. The battle

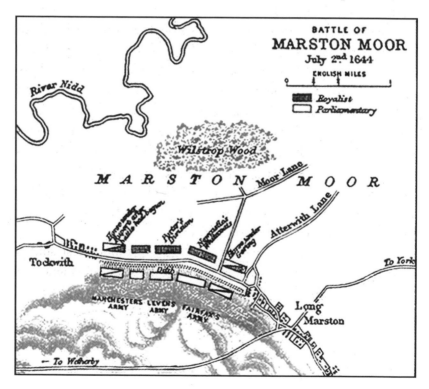

opened towards six on a summer's evening to the accompanying chords of a terrific thunderstorm, and was fought to a finish under a harvest moon. After Flodden, it was the cruelest battle ever fought on English soil, and though the chivalrous Fairfax, his lean face bleeding from a sword cut, rode up and down his lines calling on his troops to 'spare your poor deluded countrymen,' the vanquished were stubborn as the victors and died but would not surrender. In White Syke Close, a ditch encircled square on Marston Moor, a Royalist infantry regiment made a last stand, hour after hour, not thirty of their thousand surviving. These men were the Whitecoats who wore a uniform of un-dyed cloth, their boast being that they would dye it to the King's red in the blood of their enemies. The dye was their own. The trees of Wilstrop Wood, a copse a few hundred yards behind the Royalist lines, had bullets fast embedded in them when they were cut down a hundred and fifty years later, relics of the last dispersed fighting of Rupert's broken cavalry as they fled to York. It was the end of the Royalist cause in the North of England.

INVERLOCHY

FEBRUARY 2ND 1645

Four days after the disaster, Rupert on his way south met another youthful leader, the Marquis of Montrose, at the little town of Richmond. Montrose was bound for the north, set on the gigantic task of raising Scotland for the King. Disguised as a groom, he slipped across the hostile lowlands to be met near Perth by a Highlander bearing a fiery cross and the news that some royalist troops had landed from Ireland. At Blair Atholl, Montrose with a handful of clansmen met these allies. They were not 1,500 men in all, 'naked, weaponless, ammunitionless, cannonless.' But they had in Montrose a leader whose brilliance has been acclaimed unanimously by every writer on the art of war. Fortescue's verdict: 'the most brilliant natural military genius disclosed by the Civil War . . . a magician in leadership' may serve for summing up. In his Annus Mirabilis from August 1644 to August 1645 he conquered Scotland with less than two thousand men.

The Campbell clan had sided with the Covenanting lowlands; its chief, Argyll, was the head of that party throughout Scotland. A contingent of his forces, partly consisting of southern troops in modern equipment, clashed with Montrose at Tippermuir on August 31st. With a single round of ammunition for his few muskets and a hail of stones, Montrose routed them, and his men armed themselves from the abandoned stores. A fortnight later he carried Aberdeen by assault; hold it he could not and on Argyll's approach he withdrew to the hills. At Fyvie on October 20th he found the enemy with four times his numbers, all too close on his heels. Melting down the pewter mugs off the dressers of Fyvie Castle for bullets, he told his men they would have to get their powder supply from the enemy. When Argyll appeared, Montrose's people charged straight for his powder wagons; got what they wanted for their muskets and panicked Argyll's ill-led regiments into flight.

Winter was now upon them, and Argyll imagined the campaigning over, but Montrose chose this very season to carry the war into the heart of the Campbell country. Avoiding the obvious roads which were guarded, he found with the help of a guide a way through the trackless bogs of Breadalbane and surprised Argyll at Inverary. Argyll did not stay to fight; escaping southwards he left Montrose and his men to harry clan Campbell to their heart's content.

December 1644 was mild for Scotland; by January the weather turned sharper and Montrose decided to withdraw by way of Loch Etive and Glencoe. It was high time, for two forces had now been collected against him. On Friday January 30th 1645 he heard that an army of five thousand was collected to his North at Inverness, and Argyll with three thousand was to the south at Inverlochy. He himself still had only his bare fifteen hundred. At Kilcummin (now Fort Augustus) at the head of Loch Ness he took rapid stock of the situation. Was he trapped as his enemies already believed, in the narrow glens? The water lay on the one side, on the other towered the mountains. It had snowed heavily in the last weeks; the roadless stormy heights were surely impassable.

Montrose did not hesitate for long. Very early in the morning of the 31st he struck due south, following the gorge of the little river Tarff, up through the frozen crags and the drifted snow, scrambling on foot at the head of his band, his sixteen year old son at his side, into the heart of the mountains. Lost in the snowy defiles, his army disappeared utterly. Argyll's scouts could make nothing of it. Yesterday he had been the trapped prey;

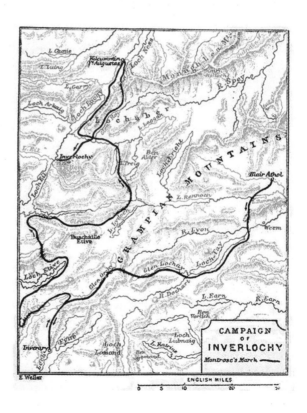

today he had simply vanished.

At the source of the Tarff, Montrose struck swiftly back towards Inverlochy, pushing through the drifted snow down Glen Roy. He and his men marched all night, without fire, without food, under a clear, cold moon. At dawn on February 1st they reached the junction of the rivers Roy and Spean and here, final stroke of daring, struck upwards over the foothills of Ben Nevis. By the red light of the winter sunset, emerging on the further Hank of the enormous range, they looked down on Argyll, crouched, all unsuspecting, at Inverlochy. It was, as John Buchan has said, 'one of the great exploits in the history of British arms.'

The battle, begun and virtually ended by the Highland charge at daybreak on the following morning, was won by shock and surprise. Even when he saw the figures in the heights Argyll had imagined a handful of stragglers, unable to believe that a body of fifteen hundred men could have disappeared into the mountains in midwinter and emerged again alive and fighting fit.

Montrose's tragedy was that with all his flexibility and genius for arms, with all his personality and skill, he had not the resources to be anything but a gucrilla leader. And no guerilla leader can carry on indefinitely without the help of a stronger and more wealthy supporter. From February to August of that year 1645 was but a succession of daring attacks and brilliant victories, at Auldearn in May, at Alford in July, at Kilsyth in August. By the late summer Montrose was master of Scotland. But he could not hold it; he could not, as his biographer says, 'fix his conquests.' Forced at length to march south in a vain attempt to reinforce King Charles in England, he could not keep his Highlanders together and he had only a bare six hundred left to pit against six thousand in his last standing fight near the border. Even for Montrose these were impossible odds. The unbroken chain of victory ended in disaster at Philiphaugh on the Yarrow in September 1645, just a year after the initial victory at Tippermuir.

NASEBY

JUNE 14TH 1645

DUNBAR

SEPTEMBER 3RD 1650

E ven while Montrose was winning victories, King Charles was suffering final defeat. Naseby, scene of a central event in English history, lies very suitably almost in the centre of England. It is an undramatic site, but on the whole little changed since Cromwell's time, so that one may work out the battle with as much satisfaction as Carlyle did just a century ago and with the help of a good deal which has been written since. One cannot better Carlyle's description of the landscape with its 'broad, blunt, clayey masses, swelling towards and from each other, like indolent waves of a sea.' This wavelike disposition of the 'hills,' as they are flatteringly called in the district, enabled Rupert to do some clever manoeuvring before the battle so as to draw Fairfax out of the ground he had selected and make him fight on terrain of Rupert's choosing. Not that it was particularly favourable terrain

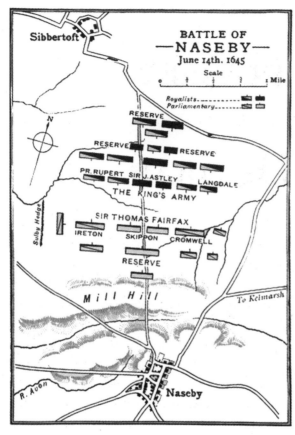

either way. The wave-like lifting and falling of the green fallow fields is such that nowhere could a uniformly f a v o u r a b l e gradient be found. The hedges have m u l t i p l i e d since that time, but one tall straggling thorn hedge, well lined with Rupert's sharpshooters, appears on the fine contemporary picture plan of Naseby in Joshua Sprigge's great folio.

The odds were heavily against the King and although Rupert's initial charge shattered the Parliamentary left wing, the right under Cromwell broke down the opposing Royalists. They were in fact not a little embarrassed by the presence of the King himself, clad in a complete suit of gilt armour which (until the present war) was to be seen in the Tower of London. One of Charles's attendants, trying to get him out of harm's way in the moment of attack, forced him to wheel his horse, a movement which was misinterpreted as an order to the whole front line and created a fatal confusion. Cromwell's second charge finally dispersed the Royalist left and he was crashing down on their undefended centre before Rupert had managed to reform his victorious cavalry and bring them back to the fight. There was nothing left for him to do but to cover the royal retreat as best he could.

It is sobering comment on the difficulty of keeping allies together that in our next battle, only five years later, Cromwell is on one side, and his old allies the Scots on the other. They had not been the only ones to dislike the execution of the King. Fairfax had resigned the chief command, and Cromwell was now the, 'Lord General', under him John Lambert and George Monk. His attempt to subdue the Scots who had brought back the young Charles II and crowned him King of their country, was not at first successful. It was a wet cold summer, supplies were supposed to come by sea from England but the storms often prevented them from landing and for weeks there were no tents. Of the 16,000 men with whom Cromwell had crossed the border in July 1650 not more than 10,000 were in a condition to fight by the end of August.

Leslie, the Scots general, had no intention of coming down from his strong position on the hill above Musselburgh to give battle to Cromwell in the strip of plain between there and the sea. Cromwell was indeed nicely trapped. Overlooked, he could neither advance nor withdraw, and when at length he decided to retreat to Dunbar on its spit of land jutting into the sea, he fully realised how easily Leslie might fall on his rear. He marched on August 31st at night and nervously enough by the fitful illumination of a rainy moon, the sea sounding on the rugged coast on his left and the hills on his right. Sure enough Leslie, keeping the main of his body on the high ground, shadowed the retreating English and attacked their rear. But at the critical moment the moon went under the clouds and Cromwell extricated his men.

Sunday September 1st found him at Hadington and ready for battle, but Leslie would not be drawn. When darkness fell, they moved again towards Dunbar. Here they were in even worse case than before, for Leslie, still on the heights, occupied Doon Hill which shuts off the short peninsular from the mainland, and sent a small force on south to Cockburnspath ('Copperspath' as the southron Cromwell has it) to man the only outlet between hills

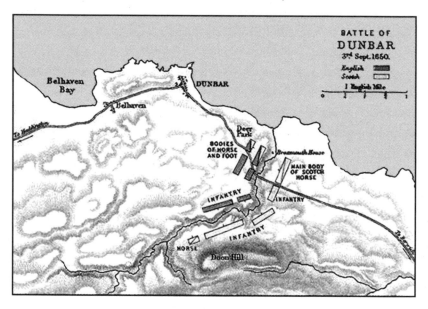

and sea leading to England and Cromwell's too distant base at Berwick. He could there either, attack Cromwell from the front and drive him into the sea or on the flank if he tried to slip through to Berwick in spite of all. His own position was pretty well unassailable at least by frontal attack. But suddenly on the Tuesday evening September 2nd Leslie shifted his whole army over towards the east end of Doon Hill and the sea. The Presbyterian ministers in the Scots camp believing that the Lord had delivered Cromwell to them, had urged him to provoke battle. He was moreover confident in the superiority of his numbers and assumed that Cromwell's men, underfed and ill, would be unfit for battle. His own men were sneezing and feverish enough after nights on the open hilltop, sheltering under the shocks of corn, tentless in the bursts of heavy summer rain.

His new position was assailable from the front, because the hill was far less steep. At its foot and between it and Cromwell's position in the plain the Brockburn ran brawling down to the sea, passable with care in two or three places, though the operation was not a wise one to attempt in full view of an enemy. Cromwell however saw that Leslie had moved his right wing too close to the sea for any difficult manoeuvring, while his left, on very steep ground, and with an impassable reach of the Brockburn in front of it, would have difficulty in going into action at all. Cromwell therefore decided to attack the right wing first, while placing his guns so that 'they might have fair play at their left wing while we were fighting their right.'

In order to do this he gave orders to cross the Brockburn in the small hours and open the attack with the first streak of the northern dawn, at about five in the morning. The weather helped: it was a 'drakie nicht full of wind and weit.' The Scots anticipated no attack. The rain put out the matches of the musketeers. The officers, tired of water dripping down their necks, left their men and huddled together in the few farmhouses of the neighbourhood. The clouds hung low and thick over moon and stars. It was inky dark.

Meanwhile, the noise blotted out by pelting rain, the English troops formed up, while Cromwell 'rid all that night through the several regiments by torchlight, upon a little Scots nag biting his lip till the blood ran down his chin.' At four o'clock he began to put his men over the brook in three places. The first three regiments surprised and put the Scots into confusion, their outposts were beaten back, their guns never got into action, and the whole English force was able to form on the nearer bank of the Brockburn.

But as the sunless morning gradually illumined the scene, it did not yet look as though the English had the best of it. Cromwell's colleagues, Lambert with the cavalry on the left and nearest the sea, and Monk with the foot in the centre advanced on the Scots position and were at first repulsed by weight of numbers, but Cromwell knowing that Leslie's left wing was helplessly pinned to its position on the uneven slopes by the play of his batteries, judged that he could safely disregard it and now flung his own cavalry of the right wing at the undefended flank of the Scots infantry, while at the same time Monk in the English centre again advanced with the foot and Lambert on the English left reformed for a second charge. Just as Cromwell had calculated, the Scots right wing of horse had had no room to manoeuvre or re-form. A second attack put their right into utter confusion, while the left never reached the action at all; and the foot in the centre were thus rapidly encircled and overwhelmed.

'The best of the enemy's horse being broken through and through in less than an hour's dispute, their whole Army being put into confusion, it became a total rout; our men having the chase and execution of them near eight miles.' So Cromwell wrote on the following day. 'We believe that upon the place and near about it were about three thousand slain. Prisoners taken: of private soldiers near ten thousand. The whole baggage and train taken, all their artillery great and small . . . You have the prospect of one of the most .signal mercies God hath done for England.'

Dunbar is the last of the great pitched battles fought on British soil, though there was to be brilliant skirmishing yet in Scotland, and some clever strategy in the '45. Cromwell's final victory over King Charles's remnants at Worcester was an efficient strategic operation. Cromwell, whose sense of a phrase and gratitude to the Almighty knew very little proportion, called it a 'crowning mercy,' though in fact it was more like a foregone conclusion. The scene of the encircling of the Royalists is very clearly to be made out in the flat green meadows where the Severn joins the Teme at Worcester and the site may be surveyed from the rising ground of Powick just outside the town. The church tower of Powick is spattered over all its southern face with musket shot, but the scars are ten years older than the battle of Worcester. They date from a skirmish at the very beginning of the Civil Wars when Prince Rupert was recruiting in the district. Thus with singular completeness, the wars began and ended in the same place.

Only once again was England the scene of fighting, when in 1685, the Duke of Monmouth landed at Lyme Regis and with his small professional band and his wild following of west country lads marched on London, to be met and utterly defeated on Sedgemoor. The expressive name tells its own story of marshy waste land; one may still see the thin strips of water which divide it, called 'fines' in the local speech, a name which rang an unexpected knell to 'King' Monmouth who had been told by a fortune teller he would die by the Rhine. There was only one bad moment for King James's men, when the rebels surprised their camp at night. The presence of mind of the second in command saved the situation which had found the commander in chief at a loss. But then the King's second in command at Sedgemoor was called John Churchill, and would in course of time be made Duke of Marlborough.

KILLIECRANKIE
July 27th 1689
CULLODEN
August 16th 1746

The last battles fought in our internal wars were in the Highlands where the ancient loyalties died very hard. In John Graham of Claverhouse, Viscount Dundee, the Stewart party found a leader second only to his great uncle Montrose in strategic insight and the management of the quarrelsome clans. 'Bonnie Dundee', or more graphically 'Black John of Battles,' was an opponent whom King William III did not underestimate. The army which he sent against him was led by a Scot of Highland extraction, General MacKay, a soldier of considerable talent, to whom the invention of the fixed bayonet is ascribed. His troops, mostly Lowland Scots, were well equipped and outnumbered Dundee's untrained horde by two to one. But the ground, with so dexterous a fighter as Dundee, was likely to be of his choosing and it was in the Highlands that MacKay had to seek out his enemy.

Towards the end of July he left Edinburgh, crossing the Forth at Stirling on the 24th; two days later at Dunkeld he heard that Dundee was at Stroan, probably making for Blair Castle. Sending on an advance guard to hold the narrow pass of Killiecrankie, MacKay followed with all speed. At Pitlochry on the following morning, Saturday 27th, he heard that his subordinates had failed to man the pass. Where Dundee was nobody seemed to know, MacKay's scouts had seen no sign of him, and thought it improbable that he was already at Blair Castle a mile or two beyond the pass. On this information MacKay took his unhappy decision to march up the narrow defile of Killiecrankie Dundee who had in fact spent the previous night at Blair Castle, was certainly lucky in MacKay's deplorable scouting.

From Pitlochry the road, such as it was, wound steadily uphill, the river Garry cascading tumultuously down on the left, the huge heather-covered mountains, towering up to three thousand feet on each side. Wide at first, the pass narrows to a gorge, then, as the course of the Garry turns almost at a right angle to the west, broadens out again, the road running on towards Blair Castle, with the Garry just below it and Ben Vrakie overhanging it on the right.

The place was perfect for an ambush and MacKay's troops marched at the alert as the hills closed in, cutting them off by their impenetrable shade from the burning July sun. How warm and reassuring must that sun have felt on the faces of MacKay and his men as they emerged at length beyond the gorge: there had been no ambush. The road to Blair Castle was empty, the

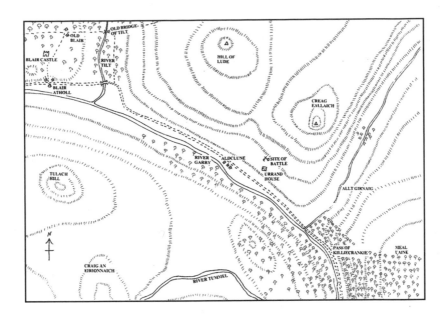

hills – green still with the heather not yet out – wrapped in the thick silence of summer.

What was it that suddenly made MacKay look up to his right hand? The stealthy rustling of the heather or the sense of unseen eyes on him? All along the slope, lifting cautious, excited heads against the skyline was the Highland host. The hill was alive.

MacKay halted. Silent, the Highlanders watched the prey. Dundee exploiting the dominating power of his personality to hold back his impetuous troops, wanted not an ambush but a pitched battle, forcing MacKay to stand and fight with the hills above and the Garry at his back. MacKay made the best of the situation, deployed his men in the flat ground with their backs to the river, and placed his strongest troops in the centre. He knew he had the advantage of numbers, and while the centre held the Highland charge, the wings, outflanking Dundee's smaller force on both sides, could close in and encircle them.

Dundee appreciated the arrangement as soon as he saw it. He thinned his line, spreading his Highlanders further and further across the brow of the hill. MacKay, puzzled, thinned his own line to three deep only and extended it again to outflank Dundee. To his dismay the bobbing heads on the skyline, not very clearly distinguished, moving here and there among the heather, now again stretched as far as his own line. Dundee realizing that encirclement by outflanking was the essential danger, had conceived of the brilliant, unorthodox ruse, of having no centre at all. He calculated rightly that his two extended wings would drive the enemy into the Garry or roll them up on to their own centre, before MacKay could appreciate or could take advantage of the fact that the Highland host was split in two.

Meanwhile the dazzling sun shone straight into the Highlanders' eyes and Dundee let it be known that when it slipped behind the distant enormous ridge of Schehallion, and only then, he would give the order for attack. The long wait had its effect in fraying the nerves of the troops below in the valley, and when at last the shining rim disappeared and the heather leapt into life, the battle did not last for long. 'There was no regiment or troop with me that did not behave like the vilest cowards,' wrote MacKay to the King twenty-four hours later. But in fact he had been completely out-generalled. Better armed and more numerous than the half-naked troops who came yelling down the face of the mountain, barelegged, bare armed, brandishing their short swords, the southerners were appalled by the fearful afternoon of waiting, by the strangeness of the spot, the thought of the Garry tearing over its rocks just behind them, above all by the sight of so much flashing steel. Their first volley of shot made no impression on the loose mass of the Highland charge, and when they came to abandon their muskets, they could not in their haste screw their bayonets into position. Moreover their line, absurdly thin, caved in at a dozen places at the first impact.

What happened was little less than the annihilation of MacKay's army; some were drowned in the Garry, others trapped trying to escape through the bottleneck of Killiecrankie. MacKay himself according to his own account was, in the twinkling of an eye, abandoned on the field.

But for one chance Killiecrankie had been a sad day for King William. One of the bullets had found a mark – by no means the silver one rumoured to be the only kind fatal to Dundee. Wounded in the thigh, in the initial charge, he had been carried aside into the heather and had there bled to death, while his followers gained the most signal victory ever won by Highlands over Lowlands.

It availed them nothing. In London there was anxious talk of the means to raise a new army against the formidable clans. 'Armies are needless,' said King William, a man of few words, 'the war is over with Dundee's life.'

It was over, more or less, for King William III but it was not over for the Highlands, not for another fifty years, not until the extinction of the Stewart cause at Culloden. The extraordinary rising of the 45, saw the most spectacular march into England of any Highland host; they turned back at Derby not because they feared military defeat, but because the English while they could hardly be enthusiastic about George II were unexpectedly loyal. In the Duke of Cumberland, George's soldier son, the English army had a leader of remarkable popularity. He was young, efficient, and much fêted by his troops under the pet name of Billy. The Highlands were to know him as Butcher Cumberland. It was another and, unhappily an equally justified point of view. (He had with him a sizeable contingent. Hessian troops, an introduction of foreign' soldiers into Great Britain which no monarchs before the Hanoverians would have dared to effect. Or perhaps Hessians did not count as foreigners, being treated by their amiable rulers as so much saleable cattle. (Their graves stretch across Europe and America in the track of every eighteenth century army.) On Cumberland's staff was a Captain James Wolfe who twelve years later with the help of Highland troops and in the name of united Britain was to be the victor of Quebec.

Prince Charles Edward, although he had withdrawn across the border and across the Forth to the safety of the Highlands, had been victorious in every engagement he had yet fought. Lord George Murray, the effective commander of the Highland host, who had shown himself a skillful strategist, seems to have made his first mistake at Culloden. Cumberland placed a garrison at Perth and pushed boldly into the Highlands. Crossing Spey, he garrisoned Inverness and celebrated his twenty-fifth birthday at Nairn on April 15th, 1746. Here, on the ensuing night, Murray thought he could surprise him, but the English host was neither so drunk nor so watchful as had been anticipated

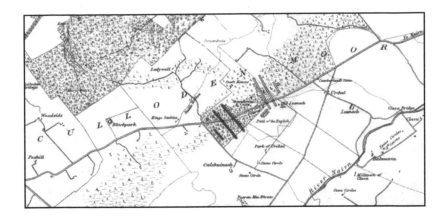

and the Highlanders exhausted themselves with a long night march to no purpose. Dispirited and outnumbered they were no match for Cumberland's forces on the following day. Moreover previous experience had at last taught the southern troops how to withstand a Highland charge. Cumberland's men were instructed to attack not their own assailant but the assailant of the man on their right. The Highland with his targe on his left arm, was defenceless on this side.

Culloden Moor, the scene of this last and final defeat of the Celtic north by the Anglo-Saxon, is a site as beautiful as it is tragic, with the desolate moor under a wild sky and the long graves of the clans buried in the places where they fell. With it the tale of fighting on British soil comes to end, to re-open in a different element close on two hundred years later when those few who, in the skies above this island saved the civilization of the world, outfought and out manoeuvred the German attack and *'left the quivering air signed with their honour.'*

List of Maps

Page 6 Map showing the chief places and battlefields mentioned in the text. Specially drawn by P O'Keefe and taken from the original edition, published by Collins, 1940.

Page 19 Map showing the Battle of Senlac (Battle of Hastings) on 14th October 1066, between the Norman army under William the Conqueror and the English army led by Harold Godwinson, taken from *A Literary & Historical Atlas of Europe* (New York, E.P. Dutton & Co, Ltd, 1910).

Page 29 Map of the Battle of Falkirk, 18th Century, origin unknown.

Page 33 Map shows the Battle of Bannockburn on 20th June, 1314, between Robert Bruce of Scotland and Edward II of England, taken from *A Literary & Historical Atlas of Europe* (New York, E.P. Dutton & Co, Ltd, 1910).

Page 38 Detail from a map of Hertfordshire showing the site of the Battle of Barnet. Map probably by H. Woutneel, c. 1602.

Page 40 Map of the Battle of Tewkesbury taken from *Lancaster and York: A Century of English History (A.D. 1399–1485) (Volume II ed.)*, Oxford, United Kingdom: Clarendon Press by James Henry Ramsay (1892).

Page 41 Plan of Bosworth Field, 1485. An engraving taken from W. Hutton's *The Battle of Bosworth Field*, 1814.

Page 44 Map of the Battle of Flodden Field taken from *A Literary & Historical Atlas of Europe* (New York, E.P. Dutton & Co, Ltd, 1910).

Page 51 Map of the Battle of Edgehill, taken from *A Literary & Historical Atlas of Europe* (New York, E.P. Dutton & Co, Ltd, 1910).

Page 54 Map of the Battle of Marston Moor taken from Samuel Rawson Gardiner's *School Atlas of English History* (Longmans, Green and Co, 1914).

Page 58 Map of the Campaign of Inverlochy, origin unknown.

Page 62 Map of the Battle of Naseby from *A Literary & Historical Atlas of Europe* (New York, E.P. Dutton & Co, Ltd, 1910).

Page 64 Map of the Battle of Dunbar taken from Samuel Rawson Gardiner's *School Atlas of English History* (Longmans, Green and Co, 1914).

Page 71 Map of the Battle of Killiecrankie. Origin unknown.

Page 75 Map of the Battle of Culloden. Origin unknown.